PLAY Guitar TODAY

Arthur and Graham Butterfield

Gordon Lightfoot, Canadian songwriter and guitarist.

Hamlyn
London . New York . Sydney . Toronto

Musical consultant/ Series editor
Arthur Butterfield

Designers
Sackville Design Ltd.

Picture Credits
Front cover: London Features International; *Back cover;* Top left, London Features International; Top right, courtesy Island Music; Bottom left, courtesy Tom Sheehan/CBS Records; Above centre, London Features International; Bottom centre, courtesy Terry Lott/CBS Records; Bottom right, London Features International; Page 43, courtesy Evolution; Page 52, courtesy RCA Records; Pages 30, 35, 48 & 55, courtesy Tom Sheehan/CBS Records; Pages 29 & 40 courtesy CBS Records; Page 59, David Redfern Photography; Page 38, Jazz Music Books; Pages 8, 9 & 25, courtesy Norlin Music (UK) Ltd. & Sampson Tyrrell Ltd.; Pages 4-5, Mike Gee; Pages 1, 2-3, 16, 23 (top), 26, 27, 32, 36, 44 (bottom left), 50 (bottom), 57 & 60, London Features International.

Pop consultant:
Bob Kenrick

Designed and produced by Intercontinental Book Productions
Copyright © 1979 Intercontinental Book Productions

Printed in Spain.
Deposito Legal B-12.051-1979

CONTENTS

Left: *America are three guitar-playing vocalists who perform the blander type of songs.*

INTRODUCTION

SO YOU have decided to take up the guitar! OK, you've made a great choice, so don't let anybody put you off by saying how difficult it is.

Of course it's difficult. No instrument is easy to *master*. But we guitarists are luckier than most: we can make a sound that's easy on the ears even after the first few minutes. After a few days you'll be able to play simple things *really well*. You don't have to take our word for it — try it for yourself and see. And just give thanks that you weren't drawn to the violin or the French horn. Some of those guys still make nasty noises after a year's hard practice.

If you really want to be an acceptable guitar picker this book will show you how. You won't have to wear your fingers to the bone practising six hours a day. And you won't find pages of dreary scales to bore you to death. But you mustn't expect right away to become a threat to Eric Clapton, John Martyn or Segovia. They're out of your league for the time being.

A word about the arrangement of this book, and then we can get down to business. All the guff — the advice about buying guitars, tuning, stringing, music theory (very little of that, we promise you) — will be kept as brief as possible. The key to success is action, and the sooner you get down to playing, the sooner you'll enjoy it.

You can skip some, most, or none of the text. It depends on how much you want to get out of the book. There are plenty of diagrams, pictures, photos, and songs so that you can't help getting some of the action right away. It might be a good idea, when your fingers get tired or sore (and they surely will at first, if you're working properly), or you just want a change from strumming, to read some of the text. It's all meaningful and said as clearly and briefly as possible. The more you read and digest, the easier it will be to play.

Practice is sometimes regarded as a dirty word. If that's how you feel about it, we apologize for mentioning it. But practice simply means *work,* and some work can be quite pleasant. We have all had to practise at some time to learn to eat, to make love, to ride a bike or drive a car. And look what that did for us! You *must* play today and *every day*. If you've got only 15 minutes a day to spare, *play every day*. It will do far more for you than a solid two hours on Sunday and nothing else for the rest of the week. After a while you won't want to put the thing down and they'll have to drag you to your meals.

Left: *A lively set from contemporary folk group Magna Carta. They have varied their line-up over the years but still harmonize perfectly on stage.*

WHAT KIND OF GUITAR?

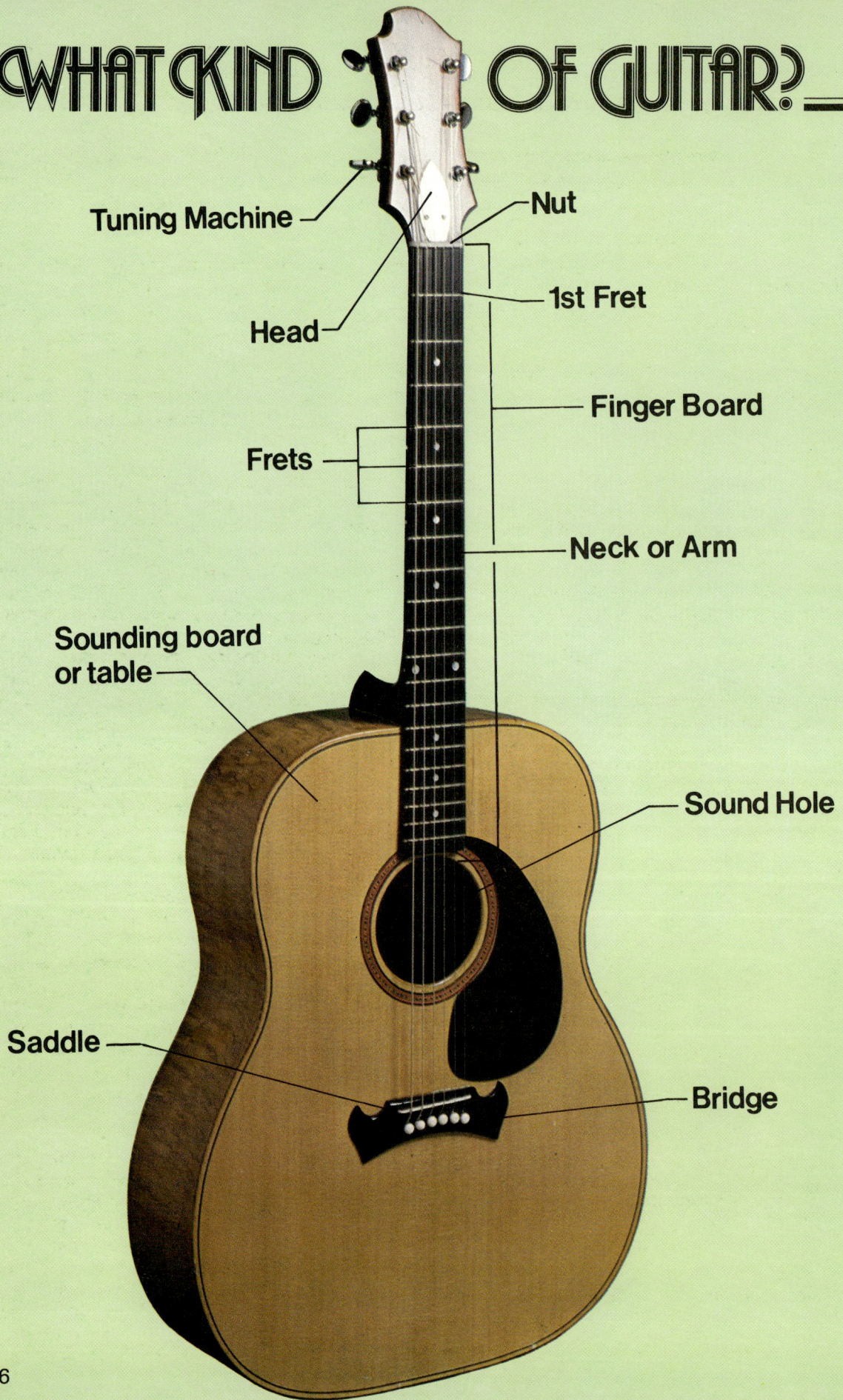

Tuning Machine

Nut

Head

1st Fret

Finger Board

Frets

Neck or Arm

Sounding board or table

Sound Hole

Saddle

Bridge

SOME OF you may know guitars like the back of your hand, even if you've never owned or played one. If so, skip this section.

This is for those of you who look in a music shop window and are confronted with serried ranks of gleaming instruments at terrifying prices and wonder where to start.

Your best bet is to take a knowledgeable friend along with you. Tell him how much or how little you are prepared to spend and what kind of music you want to play, and let him do the rest. If you have no knowledgeable friends, this is the breakdown.

Basically, as far as this book is concerned, the guitar has six strings. (You'll meet others with 12, 5, 4 and other combinations of strings. But master the conventional 6-string first and you'll find later that the others will come easy). The two main kinds of guitar are *acoustic* and *electric* (electric guitars may be solid or semi-acoustic).

Acoustic guitars usually have a round sound hole in the middle of the body and make their own sound when the strings are plucked or struck. Solid electric guitars are made out of a solid block of wood and have no sound hole. They make almost no sound of their own and are always used with amplifiers and separate speakers.

Cello guitars, a less common type, may be acoustic or amplified. Some are semi-acoustic — these are always played amplified but they do produce enough sound of their own for practice purposes. Cello guitars are easily recognized by the metal tail-piece, and the 'f'-shaped holes on either side of the bridge.

Acoustic guitars may be nylon-strung, in which case they are played with the fingers. These are used mainly by classical guitarists (such as Segovia and John Williams), and folksingers and flamenco players.

Acoustic guitars may also have steel instead of nylon strings. Such guitars usually have reinforced necks because of the extra pull of the strings, and a scratch plate along the edge of the sound hole to protect the surface of the instrument from the action of the pick. This type of guitar is favoured by some folksingers and most country music and bluegrass players, and is played either with a single pick (plectrum) or individual thumb and fingerpicks.

Solid and cello guitars may be played with a plectrum or with the fingers. Most rock musicians use solid guitars; cello guitars are quite often found in dance bands or sometimes jazz bands.

If you are a complete beginner, it might be as well to start off with a nylon-strung acoustic, although this type of guitar is not really suitable for flatpicking. But a strong point in its favour is that it is easy on the fingers and easy on the pocket. And don't worry about whether to play with a plectrum or with the fingers. You'll learn both together as you go along.

When it comes to talking turkey and adding up the cost, you'll find that no musical instrument is cheap. But a really good guitar, properly looked after, is an investment because it grows more valuable with age. And anyway, it's a darn sight cheaper than most other musical instruments of similar quality.

Among the nylon-strung acoustics — the so-called 'classical' or 'Spanish' guitars — there are some real beauties to be had for about £100 or so, most of them Japanese. But you don't have to splash out that sort of money to begin with. You just might get fed up with the thing after a short while and that would be pounds down the drain.

On the other hand, any instrument whose new price is less than about £30 is frankly not worth buying. It then becomes merely an expensive toy that makes an unpleasant sound and is just about unplayable.

Here's a tip for left-handers. If you feel you must, you can always re-string your *acoustic* guitar to reverse the normal order of the strings, then put your right hand on the fingerboard and strum with your left. You can't do this with *electric* guitars because of pickup problems, but you can buy special left-handed electrics. However, it is only fair to point out that many natural left-handers (including the authors) play right-handed guitar with no difficulty at all.

Opposite: *Parts of the guitar. This is a steel-strung, flat-top acoustic guitar. The type of guitar you choose depends on the type of music you want to play and how much you can afford to pay.*
Above: *When buying a guitar squint down the neck to check that it is straight and not warped.*

Classical acoustic guitar
(nylon-strung)

Flat-top acoustic guitar
(steel-strung)

Semi-acoustic cello guitar

Solid electric guitar

BITS AND PIECES

THERE IS no need for a rundown on the various bits and pieces of the guitar. The pictures show you almost everything you need to know. Note that the machine-heads (the 'pegs' for tightening and loosening the strings) vary according to whether the guitar is nylon- or steel-strung.

Two common faults in cheap guitars are a warped neck and a high action. To check for the first fault, squint down the length of the fingerboard or run a straight edge along it. If it curls uphill and down dale, or if it twists or leans to left or right, throw it out. The *action* describes the height of the strings above the frets. Make sure that all the strings are easy to press down and have little distance to travel, especially where they approach the sound hole.

You may come across a guitar whose neck is slightly warped but not badly enough to make it unplayable. If the action is low, you should check each string by playing it on every fret. Any rattles or buzzing noises may indicate a hefty refretting operation, so pass the instrument by.

Incidentally, the word *fret* refers both to the

The head of the guitar and the tuning machines differ according to the type of instrument in use.
Below: This head is part of a nylon-strung guitar.
Below right: Flat-top head of a steel-strung guitar.

metal strips that cross the fingerboard at regular intervals, *and* to the spaces between each strip.

Bridging the Gap

The bridge of a guitar is a small but highly important piece of wood with a plastic or metal 'saddle' (the top part on which the strings rest). The bridge holds one end of the strings and determines their tension and action. On acoustic guitars there are two types of bridges:

(1) the classical type with horizontal string holes through which the strings are threaded and looped

(2) the flat top type with vertical string holes through which the strings are fed and hooked under the belly of the guitar; the strings are then held in position by wooden or plastic pins called 'bridge pins'.

Some types of electric and cello guitars have a movable or 'floating' bridge. The strings pass over this and are connected to a metal tailpiece fixed at the end of the guitar.

Some flat guitar bridges have adjustable bridge saddles. With these you can easily raise or lower the action of the strings and so adjust the volume level. If you want greater volume, raise the saddle; if you want less, lower it.

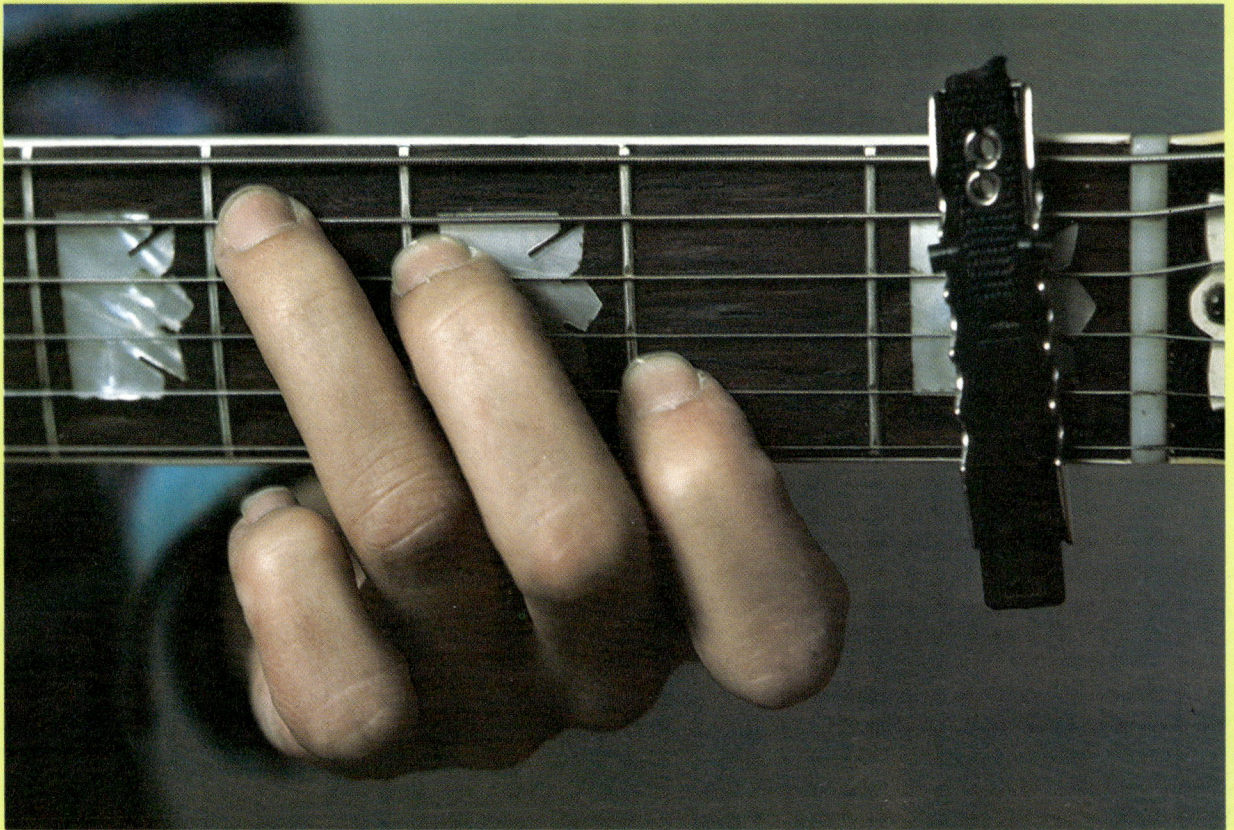

The Capo, or How to Play in any Key Without Really Trying

The capo is an extremely useful little device that will immediately enable you to play in almost any key with the minimum of effort. Shunned like the plague by classical guitarists and ignored by rock specialists, it is widely used by country and flamenco guitarists, and is the busker's boon.

The capo consists of a flat metal or rubber bar that fits across all six strings of the guitar at once, and is usually held in place by elastic or by a screw attachment. Capos come in many forms and at varying prices. Their effect is to shorten the effective length of the sounding strings and thus raise the pitch (sound). If, for example, you clamped your capo across the first fret of your guitar, the capo would then in effect be the new nut. Every note would sound half a tone higher in pitch, so that if you were to finger a C Major chord with the capo in that position the sound would actually be that of C sharp.

The day may come when you find yourself accompanying a recalcitrant vocalist who persists in singing solely in E flat. Don't despair, however. Merely slide your capo up to the third fret and play happily away in C shapes!

Above: *The capo has been clamped across the first fret and the C-shape chord now becomes C sharp.*
Below: *The saddle, which rests on the bridge, supports the strings and provides the tension.*

STRINGING ALONG

LIKE MOST other things in this life, guitar strings do not last forever: occasionally they break, or they begin to lose their resonance, and so have to be replaced. Guitars are built to take either nylon or steel strings, but never both. Nylon strings are found on classical and flamenco guitars; steel strings are used on flat top and all kinds of electric guitars. On a nylon-strung guitar the three top strings (the thinnest — EBG) are made of smooth nylon, whereas the three bottom strings (the thickest — DAE) are of nylon wrapped with a very fine bronze wire. This makes them look like steel strings. But because they are actually nylon strings, you must never try to replace them with steel strings or you'll end up with an armful of very bent guitar. A guitar built for nylon strings will never stand up to the pull of steel strings.

The strings of a steel-strung guitar are not all the same. The two thinnest strings, E and B, are made of smooth steel, whereas the other four, G,

D, A and E, have steel cores with either chrome or bronze windings.

Replacing a Nylon String

Loosen the string and unwind it from the tuning peg. Next unthread the string through the small loop or eye that should be on the sound hole side of the bridge. You will then be able to pull the string clear of the bridge. Take the plain end (the one without the nylon eye) of the new string, thread it through the hole in the bridge (on the sound hole side) and pull it through until the nylon eye is just a little more than a centimetre from the bridge. Thread the other end of the string through the eye and pull tight. That's one end of the string fixed. [Some nylon-strung guitars take strings that *don't* have eyes. So if you have any problems ask the assistant in the music shop for advice.] Now you have to attach the

other end of the string to the tuning peg. You do this by threading about 7½ centimetres of the string through the small hole in the tuning peg and turning the peg until the tightened string reaches its correct pitch. To achieve this, turn the bottom three strings *away* from you, and the top three strings *towards* you.

Replacing a Steel String

Loosen the string and unwind it from the tuning peg. To detach the other end from the bridge, pull out the plastic or wooden pin that holds the string to its hole in the bridge, then lift the string out. *Never* try to take the bridge pin out before removing the string from the tuning peg.

To fit a new string, take the end with the small steel bead attached to it and feed it into the hole in the bridge. Make sure that the bead fits snugly under the bridge, inside the belly of the guitar,

and cannot be pulled straight out. Then secure the string by replacing the bridge pin. Take the other end of the string and thread it through the small hole in the tuning peg. Leave enough slack to be able to wind the peg shaft at least four times before the string begins to take the strain. Before tightening the string to tune it, make sure that it is lying in the correct groove in the nut. Turn the bottom three pegs *away* from you and the top three *towards* you, to tighten the strings to the correct pitch.

To preserve your strings from sweat and dust always wipe them down with a dry cloth after use – this will lengthen their useful life.

Opposite page: *Plastic or wooden pins hold steel strings in place on the bridge. Note the eye at the end of the string (far left). This is fed into the bridge and the string is secured by the pin (near left).*
Below: *Threading the sixth string through the peg.*

WELL, NOW that you've begged, borrowed, or bought your guitar you'll be dying to get cracking. But before you can play a note you'll have to learn to tune the thing. There are several ways of doing this. If you have a piano or other keyboard instrument (such as a piano accordion or an organ), you're home and dry. Possessing such an instrument, you should have no difficulty in picking out the notes E A D G B E in ascending order in the middle register of the keyboard. These notes correspond to the six 'open' strings of the guitar (that is, the strings played without pressing them down with the left hand on any of the frets), starting with the thickest and deepest sounding string and on up to the thinnest one with the highest pitch.

For those of you who can read music, don't be thrown by the fact that the guitar sounds an octave lower than it should: guitar music is written an octave higher than the sound of the notes for ease of reading in the treble clef.

Tuning to a Keyboard

To tune the strings to each note, pick each string one at a time with your thumb or finger. If it sounds *lower* than the keyboard note, turn the corresponding machine head to *tighten* that particular string. If it sounds *higher* than the piano or organ key, turn the same machine head the other way, to *loosen* the string. Keep on doing this until you get as near to the right sound as you can. You'll find that after a few days you'll be quite expert at it.

It's always easier to get spot-on sound by tightening rather than loosening a string. So when tuning, loosen the string rather more than you need to, then 'tighten up' to the required sound. You'll also find to your dismay that nylon strings when new tend to stretch quite a lot. So don't get downhearted if at first you can't keep the thing in tune for more than a few minutes at a time. The strings will settle down in a day or two and the job of tuning will grow beautifully less.

Tuning to a Pitchpipe

If you have no keyboard to tune to, you'll probably have to invest in a pitchpipe. This is a small mouth instrument that looks like six short flutes joined together — one for each string of the guitar. You'll see the six notes — E A D G B E — stamped on the pipes. All you have to do is blow each pipe in turn and tune the guitar as before. Pitchpipes are cheap, but they do have an unfortunate habit of going out of tune fairly quickly and so have to be replaced.

Tuning with a Tuning Fork

Another way of tuning is to use a tuning fork. This will never go out of tune, but it vibrates only to one note. The note is usually marked on it. To make it easy, take one tuned to E. Start the fork vibrating by striking it on something solid. Then rest the fork on the sounding board of your guitar to amplify the sound. Hum that note or whistle it so as to remember it while tuning. Then tune the sixth string (the thickest) to that note.

Tuning the Strings to Each Other

Whether you use a keyboard, a pitchpipe, or a tuning fork, you should always check the results by tuning the six strings to each other. This is how you do it.

Let us suppose that your sixth string (E) is now in tune, by one means or another. Now put a finger on the 5th fret of the sixth string and pluck it. Then tune the *fifth* string to that sound by plucking it and loosening or tightening the string as appropriate. When you've done that, your open fifth string (A) will be in tune. Do the same with the fourth string (D), tuning it to the fifth string, fretted at the 5th fret. Carry on and tune the third string (G) to the fretted fourth. Then tune the second (B) to the third, but this time fret the third string at the *4th* fret. Then move back to the 5th fret to tune the first string (E) to the second.

When you 'fret' a string, you press down in the open space just behind the metal fret. Press firmly and make sure that the note rings out clearly — there must be no muffling or buzzing.

Gauging Your Strings

Steel strings come in four different *gauges* (thicknesses): heavy, medium, light and extra light. If you're after a solid, no-nonsense, booming bass, it's the heavy gauge for you. Medium gauge strings serve the best of both worlds: you can get a fairly solid beat from them, and at the same time they don't get in the way of fast 'licks' and sparkling solo work. Light strings are designed mainly for virtuoso solo playing.

Opposite, reading left to right from the top: *When tuning one string against another, tune the sixth string (picture 1) to a known E note then fret that string at the fifth fret (2) and tune the next string to the sound. Tune the fourth string to the fifth in the same way (3) and the third to the fourth (4). Tune the second to the third by fretting the* fourth *fret (5), then revert to the fifth fret (6), fretting the second string to tune the first.*

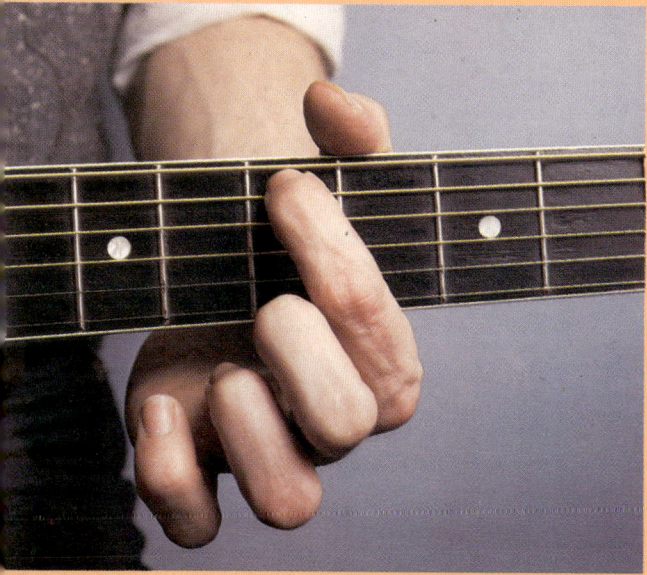

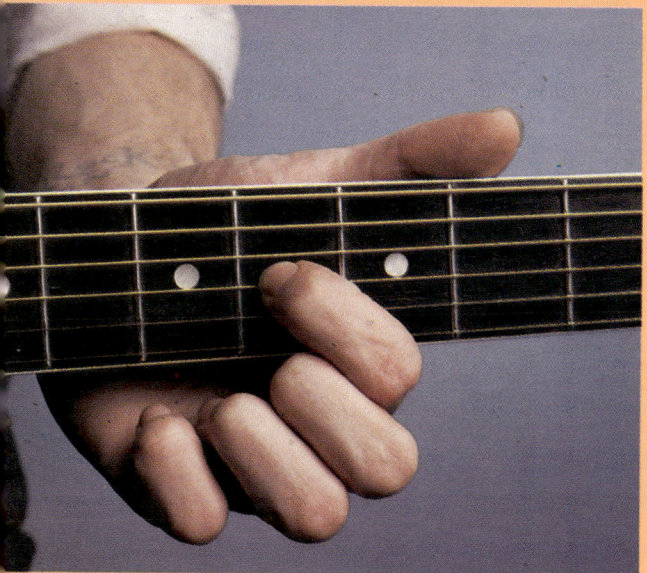

FINGERS AND NAILS

IN ORDER to make it clear which hand we are dealing with, the fingers of your left hand are coloured and those of your right hand are called by their usual names.

With the left hand you use only the four fingers for fretting purposes. In some jazz and rock techniques the thumb is curled over the sixth string but at this stage that should not be necessary. The fingers are coloured red (index), green (middle), purple (ring), and brown (little finger). You may find it useful to colour your nails with felt-tip pens.

You use the right hand fingers for plucking or strumming the strings. The little finger is a passenger, and if using picks it is often rested on the guitar to give additional support to the hand — sheer heresy to the classical guitarist!

The nails of your left hand should be trimmed as short as possible. This allows you to press the strings down firmly without digging into the wood underneath. If you are fingerpicking on nylon strings the nails of your right hand should be reasonably long and filed smooth as glass. They are your natural picks. But if you are picking with metal or plastic picks on your fingers, or using a single flatpick, long nails can be an embarrassment and a nuisance.

Opposite: *Cat Stevens in concert.*
Above right: *The left hand with the fingernails marked with their respective colours.*
Right: *A chord (G7) being held in position.*
Below: *The thumb of the left hand in its correct classical position on the neck of the guitar.*

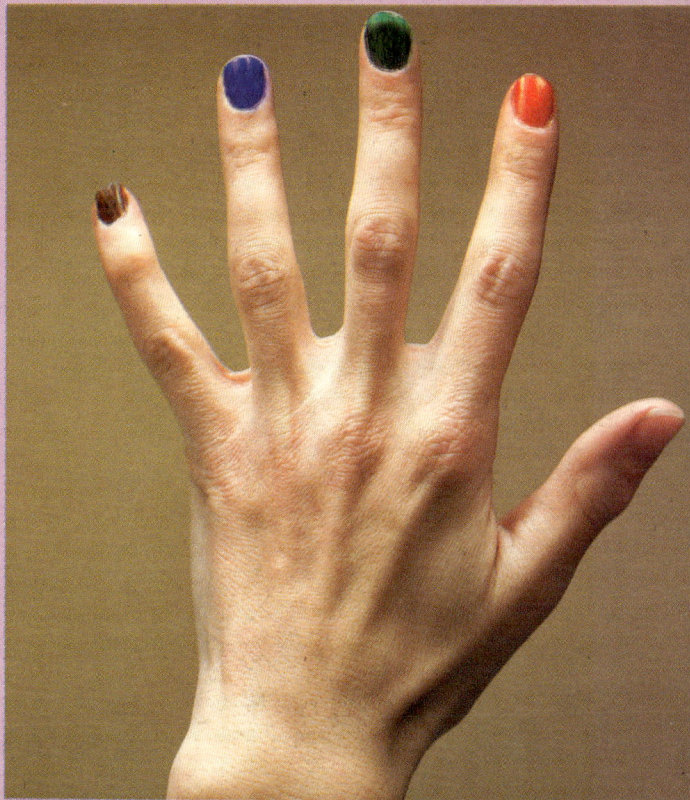

GETTING TO GRIPS WITH IT

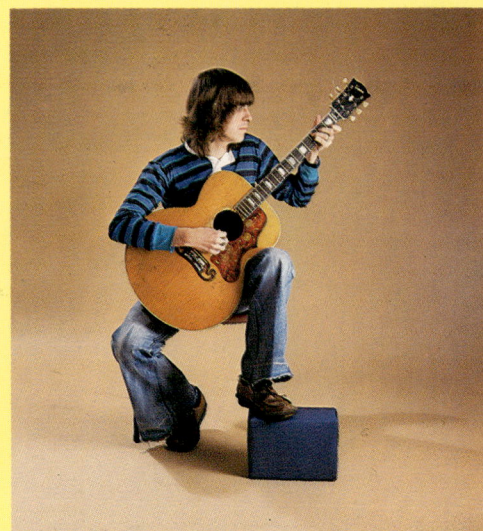

There are many ways of holding a guitar. Above: *The upright position has the guitar suspended by a strap*. Top and centre right: *Two ways of balancing the instrument on the right thigh — choose the one which is most comfortable*. Bottom right: *The classical stance, which calls for a foot-stool*.

DON'T BE afraid of your guitar. It's yours, and you should learn to love it from the start. One day, soon, it will be making beautiful music for you. Hug it close to your body. Sit down to the job at first. Later, when picking comes easy to you, you can stand and hang it from a strap around your shoulders. All classical performers and most flamenco guitarists prefer to sit down. Popular guitarists, especially on stage, almost always face their audiences standing.

Try, firstly, balancing the guitar comfortably on your left thigh, holding it almost vertically. It should cross the front of your body at an angle so that the machine heads are roughly level with your left shoulder. You can cross your left leg over your right, or support it on a small footstool or a pile of books. (If you want to play classical guitar a footstool is a must). When you get used to the feel of the thing, you can try other positions. Rest it on the other knee (as in the pictures opposite). Hang it round your shoulder from a strap. You will eventually find your own way of holding the guitar — the one most comfortable for you.

Keep your left elbow tucked in and your left forearm at right angles to the fingerboard. Keep your fingers poised just above the strings ready to press the required frets. Your left hand knuckles should be close to and parallel with the fingerboard. Ideally, your thumb should be straight, with the ball of the thumb pressing into the back of the neck of the guitar, supporting the fingers above. However, you may soon find, like many guitarists, that it is more comfortable to curl your thumb over the neck of the guitar. There's nothing wrong with this unless you're playing in the classical style.

Plucking the Strings

Your right hand produces the notes and varies their tone. Pluck the strings right over the sound hole for a normal tone. Pluck nearer the bridge and you get a taut, tinny tone. Farther up the neck the sound becomes mellower.

Place your hand with a slightly arched wrist directly over the strings. Your fingers should be slightly curved. Hang your right forearm in a relaxed way over the bulging part of the guitar. Your right-hand thumb usually plays the three lowest-sounding strings: 6, 5, and 4 (E, A, and D respectively). The third string (G) is usually played with your index finger, the second (B) with your middle finger, and the first string (E) with your ring finger. There are exceptions to these rules but only in more advanced techniques.

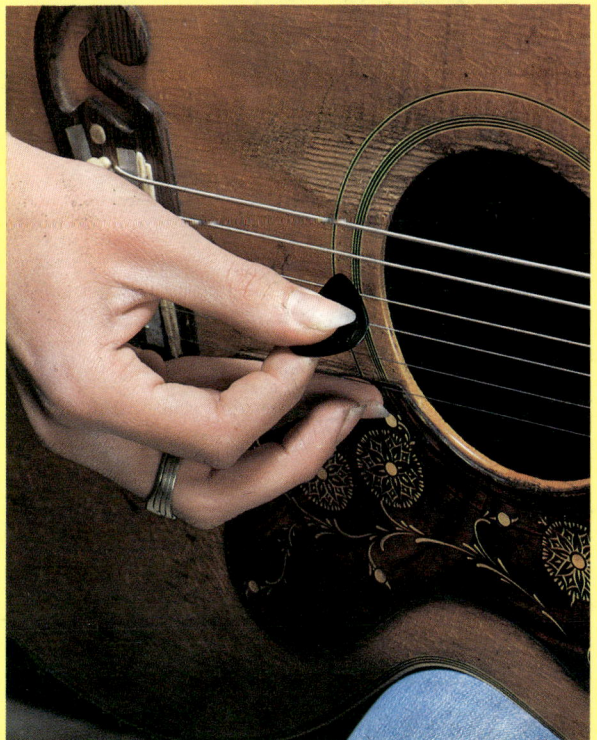

Two principal ways of picking the strings: finger-picking (top) uses direct contact between the fingers and the strings; flatpicking (above) is done with a pick or plectrum, usually on steel strings.

19

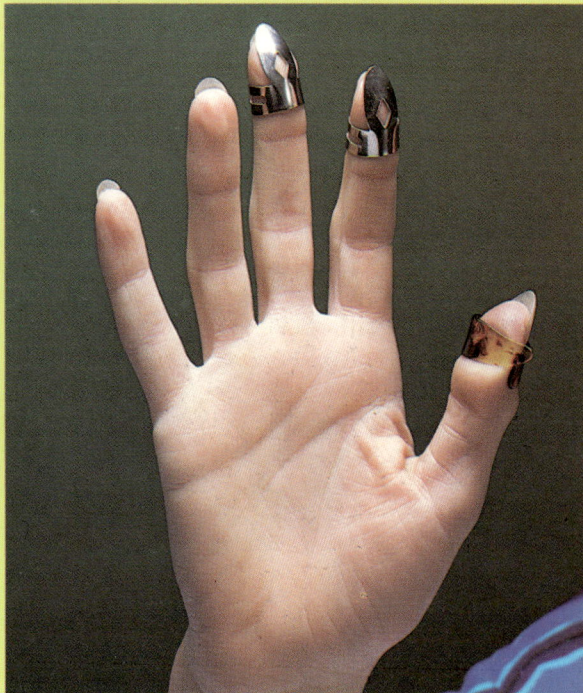

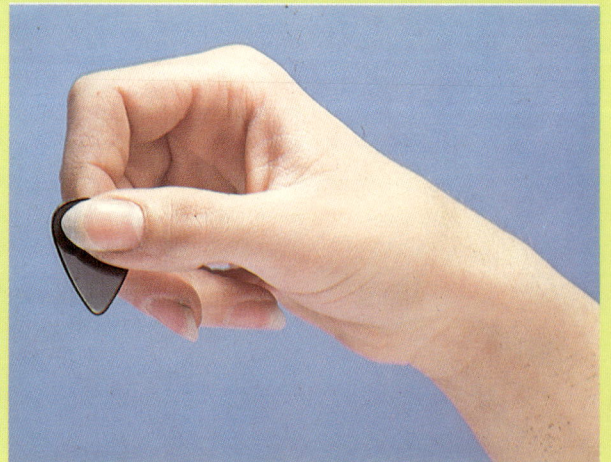

Top: *Flatpicking with metal fingerpicks. You lose some sensitivity in your fingertips but you can judge your position on the strings by supporting the hand with your little finger on the scratch plate.*
Left: *A palm view showing the picks in place on the thumb, index, and middle fingers.*
Above: *The correct way to hold the pick or plectrum; this is usually made of plastic or tortoiseshell.*

LOOK — NO MUSIC

YOU DON'T have to read music in order to be able to play it. You can start straight away to learn chords and to play them. The colour coded system — illustrated below — is the key to this. The chord diagram here is a guitarist's-eye-view of the strings and the first three frets of the guitar fingerboard. (Try looking over the fingerboard — tilting the guitar up towards you — and you will see that the diagram corresponds to your own viewpoint.) Each coloured dot shows you which string to play and where to fret it, and also which finger to use — see the picture (bottom left) for the colour coding of the left-hand fingers.

So to form the chord shown here you press the second string down at the 1st fret with your index (red) finger, and on the 2nd fret press down the first string with your ring (purple) finger and the third string with your middle (green) finger.

Your left hand is all ready to go. Now with your right hand you play all the strings that are fretted and any string with a nought (0) at the end — you are playing these strings open (unfretted). A cross (X) against a string means that you don't play or fret that string at all.

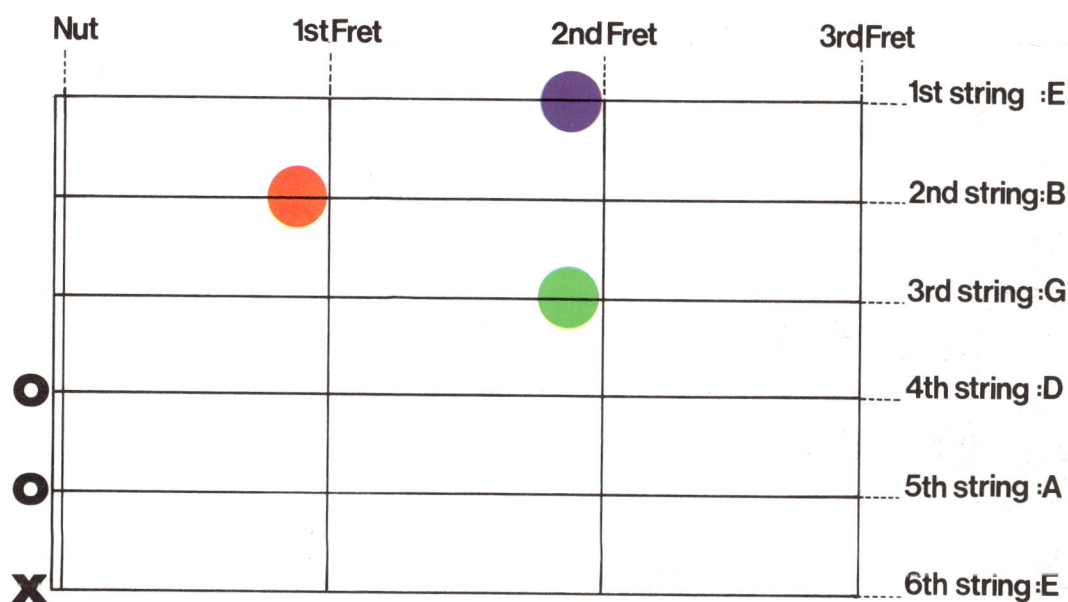

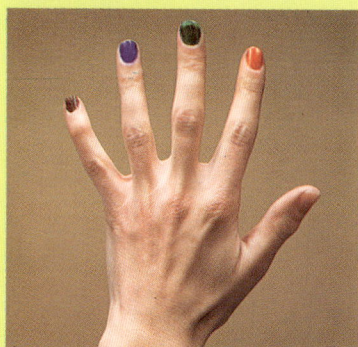

Nut	1st Fret	2nd Fret	3rd Fret	
		● (purple)		1st string : E
	● (red)			2nd string : B
		● (green)		3rd string : G
O				4th string : D
O				5th string : A
X				6th string : E

Top: *The coloured dots on the chord diagram correspond to the coloured fingertips (above). The diagram shows how a D7 chord is fingered.*
Right: *A guitarist's-eye-view of the same chord being played on the guitar fingerboard.*

CHORDS COME EASY

AND NOW you can start playing at last. You know how to hold the thing, you've tuned it, and you know the names (letters) of the six open strings. These, as you know, are six musical notes. The two outside strings (E) are the same in name but different in pitch (highness or lowness in sound). The top E (string No. 1) is 16 notes higher in pitch than the bass E (string No. 6). But if you pluck them together they should blend.

When several notes are played together they form a *chord.* Strictly and musically speaking, a chord must be made up of at least three notes played together. But for our purposes we can call any two or more notes together a chord.

Western musical notation is usually divided up into seven different whole tones. They are named after the letters of the alphabet: A B C D E F G. When they get past G they start again with A.

Chords, according to how they are formed, take names of these notes. This means you can have a C chord or an A chord or an F chord, and so on.

Chords also form families, just like human beings. A very simple and basic grouping is the three-chord family (or three-chord trick as some card-playing buskers have christened it). The three chords in each of these family units are closely related in sound, and lead naturally from one to the other.

Take a G chord for example. Its two closest buddies in the family are the chords of C and D (all three chords are illustrated below). The great advantage of the G chord family is that none of the three is particularly difficult to play.

You will also, before long, come across the word *key* in connection with music. It can, of course, mean part of the instrument itself, such

The G Chord

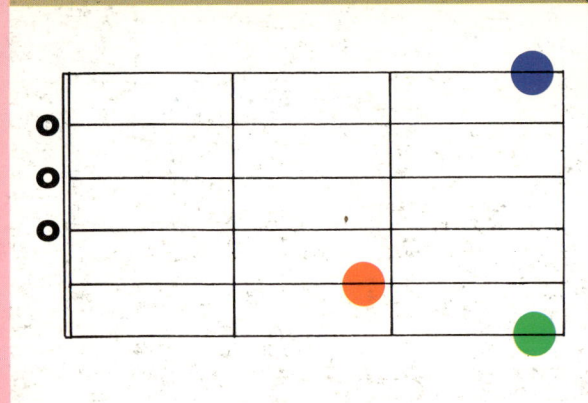

The C Chord

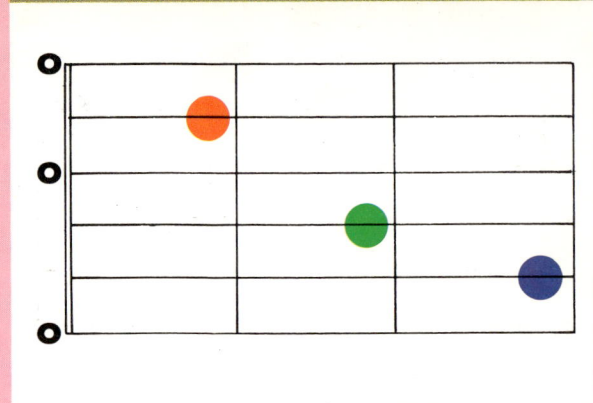

as a piano key. But in musical theory it refers to the classification of the notes of a *scale*. A scale is just a musical ladder of the seven basic tones plus an eighth tone which is a repeat of the first tone of the scale, eight tones higher or lower. You can go up or down the scale in whole tones (steps) or half tones or a mixture of both. The first and last notes of the scale (which are the same) form the *keynote,* the most important note of the scale, and all the other notes are then related to it. And so a song or a piece of music based on, say, a scale that starts and ends with G, is said to be in the key of G.

Right: *Don Williams's simple picking backs up his down to earth country songs.*
Below right: *Leo Kottke, a gifted 12-string player.*

The D Chord

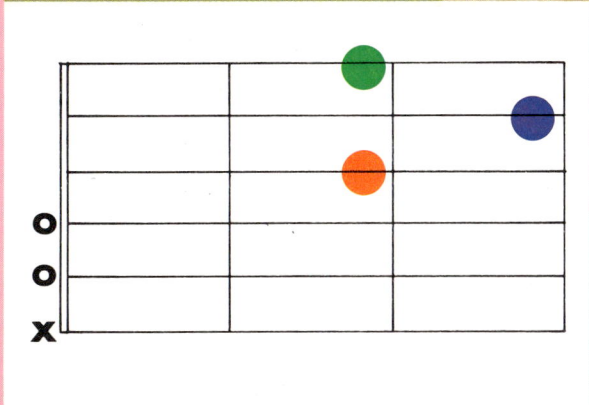

ON YOUR MARKS

NOW LET'S get down to business. Put your left-hand fingers in the position shown on page 22 for a G chord. Once you've got it without any slipping, bending, or buckling, play the chord. Don't try anything fancy with your right hand just yet. Just strum the chord through with your thumb or with a pick. (Each red stroke indicates a down strum). It's your left hand that you've got to watch here. Keep brushing down across the strings until you're pretty confident you know how to get a G chord (even without looking), and also know what it sounds like.

Now do exactly the same for the C chord. When you've got used to this, try changing back and forth, to G and then back to C. Play several strokes on each at first, then try changing from one to the other after just one stroke each time.

Now do the same for the D chord but remember not to strum the sixth string (marked 'X'). Get used to the feel and shape of it. When you're quite happy about each of the three chords individually, then play them in turn, changing from one to the other in a different order.

You may find this tricky and offputting at first, and your fingers may begin to feel sore. But keep at it. You'll soon be delighted with the way the thing starts to sort itself out, as you move almost automatically from one chord to another without thinking and without looking. And once you've mastered these three basic chords you'll be able to play a great many songs.

If, later in the book, you find the new playing techniques too tricky you can always strum through the songs once you know the chords.

1 G

/ / / / / / / / / / / / / / / / / /

2 C

/ / / / / / / / / / / / / / / / / /

C   G   C

/ / / / / / / / / / / / / / / / / /

3 D   G   D

/ / / / / / / / / / / / / / / / / /

D   C   D

/ / / / / / / / / / / / / / / / / /

G   C   D   G   D   G

/ / / / / / / / / / / / / / / / / /

AMAZING GRACE

LET'S START with an easy one: *Amazing Grace*. This is a traditional hymn dating from colonial days in America. It was popularized by Judy Collins and others, and from then on it received a new lease of life.

Remember that the red slanting strokes represent down strokes played by you. Try it with your thumb at first. Change chords on the exact word, as shown. Hold that chord all the way until you come to a new one; then change on the word again. Hum or sing along with your playing – this makes it much easier. For those of you who don't know the song the conventional musical notation is included at the bottom of the page. Pick it out on a keyboard or get a friend to play it for you and you'll soon be strumming away.

Try moving from one chord to another as smoothly as you can. Never mind how slow it is. One of the great secrets of good guitar playing is that swift and smooth movement of the left hand from one position to another.

Right and opposite: U.S. folksinger Judy Collins, an established solo singer and guitarist. Her version of Amazing Grace sent it racing up the charts.

G   C   G   D7

Amazing grace, how sweet the sound that saved a wretch like me.

G   C G   D G

I once was lost but now I'm found, was blind but now I see.

2. 'Twas grace that taught my heart to fear, and grace my fear relieved.
How precious did that grace appear, the hour I first believed.

3. Through many dangers, toils and snares we have already come.
'Twas grace that brought us safe thus far, and grace will lead us home.

4. When we've been there ten thousand years, bright shining as the sun.
We've no less days to sing God's praise than when we first begun.

5. REPEAT FIRST VERSE

Am—a—zing— grace how sweet the sound tha-t saved a wretch like me. I once was lost but now I'm found was blind but— now I see. 2. 'Twas

SLOOP JOHN B.

GETTING FED up with *Amazing Grace?* Let's try another song, *Sloop John B.* This is a traditional melody with a slightly Caribbean flavour, that became a runaway hit for the Beach Boys some years ago. It's almost as easy as *Amazing Grace.* That involved one stroke to a bar (a musical measure of time). This is slightly faster: you give one stroke of your thumb for each beat. Note that the second D chord occurs in the breathing space *after* the word 'up' – 'up' itself is part of the G chord.

Right: The Beach Boys brought to rock the loose-limbed sound of surf music from the West Coast.

G
We sailed on the Sloop John B / / / / / / / My grand father and me / / /

D
All around Na ssau to wn we did roam / / / / Went drinkin'

G   **C**   **G**
all night / / Got into a fight / / / / / / I feel so broke

D   **G**   CHORUS
up I wanna go home / / / / So hoist up the John B

Sails / / / See how the main sail sets / / / Call for the captain

D
a shore / Let me go home / / / / Let me go home / / / / /

C
Let me go home / / / / / / Yes I feel so broke up

G
I wanna go home / / / / / / / /

2. The first mate got drunk, broke into the captain's trunk
The constable had to come and take him away.
Sheriff John Stone, why don't you leave me alone?
I feel so broke up, I wanna go home.

CHORUS

3. And the cook he got the fits, he threw out all my grits
Then he took and ate up all of my corn.
Let me go home, why don't you let me go home?
Yes, this is the worst trip I've ever been on.

CHORUS

We sailed on the Sloop John B My grand fa—ther and me. All
a—round Na-ssau town we — did roam. Went drinking all night
Got in—to a fight. I feel so broke up I wanna go
home. So hoist up the John B sails See how the main sail
sets — Call for the captain a—shore let me go home. Let me go
home Let me go — home Yes I feel so broke up
I wanna go home.

TAKE IT ON THE UPBEAT

SO FAR you've learnt how to accompany songs with a steady downbeat. But this gets a bit monotonous after a time. To vary it we bring in an upbeat now and then. And to get it we just strum upwards on the *blue* stroke, lightly with the side of the thumb to start with. Remember, red strokes go *down* for a full beat; blue strokes come *up* for just half the length of time.

Let's try this new technique with *Banks of the Ohio.* This traditional old murder ballad has attracted dozens of folk and country singers, as well as pop artists like Olivia Newton John. Joan Baez has recorded one of the most compelling versions. The slow up-and-down lick on the guitar helps a lot. You should be able to manage the chord changes without too much difficulty.

Rebellious folksinger Joan Baez (right and below) sings to a strong rhythmic accompaniment.

BANKS OF THE OHIO

G   **D**

I asked my love   to take a walk,   to take a walk

              G   **C**

just a little way.   As we walked   and as we talked,

      G **D**   **G**

we spoke a-bout   our wedding day.   And onl-y say   that you'll

  D   **G**

be mine   and in no oth-er's   arms en-twine.   Down be-side

       C   **G**   **D**   **G**

where the waters flow   down by the banks   of the O-hi o.

2. I held a knife against her breast
    As into my arms she pressed.
    She cried, ''Oh Willy don't you murder me,
    I'm unprepared for eternity.''

    CHORUS

3. I wandered home 'tween twelve and one
    I cried ''My God what have I done?''
    I've killed the only woman I love
    Because she would not be my bride.

    CHORUS

I asked my love to take a walk, to take a walk just a lit-tle way. As we walk—ed and as we talk—ed We spoke a—bout our wed-ding day. CHORUS And on—ly say that you'll be mine and in no o—ther's arms en—twine. Down be—side Where the wa—ters flow down by the banks of the O—hi—o. 2. I held a

MAKING IT COUNT

HERE IS an extension of the up-and-down strum or lick. Kris Kristofferson's *Me and Bobby McGee* lends itself to this type of picking. You can fairly hear the rolling wheels as they drum along the highway to the slapping rhythm of the windscreen wipers. Take it on the slow side but keep the beat going.

ME AND BOBBY McGEE

G
Bus-ted flat in Baton Rouge   headin' for the trains,   feelin' nearly faded

D
as my jeans.   Bobby thumbed a diesel down   just before it rained,

G
took us all the way to New Or-leans.   I pulled my har-poon out from my

C
dirty red band-ana,   I was blowin' sad while   Bobby sang the blues.

G
With the windshield wipers slappin' time and   Bobby clappin'

D   **G**
hands we finally sang through every song that driver knew.

C · · · /// / · · · G · · / / //// /

Freedom's just a-nother word for nothing left to lose.

D · · · / / // · · · G · //// C / · · /

Nothing ain't worth nothing but its free.   Feelin' good was

/ · // · · · G · // · · // · · D / · · · G · ////

easy Lord when Bobby sang the blues.   Feelin' good was

/ · / · · // //// / · · · / · · · · // / · · / ////

good enough for me.   Good enough for me and Bobby Mc-Gee.

2. From the coal mines of Kentucky to the California sun, Bobby shared the secrets of my soul. Standing right beside me, Lord, through everything I done, every night she kept me from the cold. But somewhere near Salinas, Lord, I let her slip away, searching for the home I hope she'll find. But I'd give all my tomorrows for a single yesterday, holding Bobby's body close to mine.

CHORUS

Bus—ted flat in Bat—on Rouge head—in' for the trains Feel—in' near—ly
fad—ed as my jeans Bob—by thumbed a dies—el down
just be—fore it rained, Took us all the way to New Or—leans.
I pulled my har—poon out from my dir—ty red band—an—a, I was
blow—in' sad while Bob—by sang the blues. With the wind-shield wi—pers
slap—pin' time and Bob—by clap—pin' hands we final—ly Sang through eve—ry song that driv—er
knew. CHORUS Free—dom's just a—no—ther word for noth—ing left to
lose. No—thing ain't worth noth—ing but it's free.
Feel—in' good was eas—y Lord when Bob—by sang the blues. Feel—in' good was
good en—ough for me Good en—ough for me and Bob—by 'Mc—Gee.

Words and music by Kris Kristofferson. © 1969 by Combine Music Corp., (USA). Sub-published by Keith Prowse Music Pub. Co. Ltd., 138-140 Charing Cross Road, London WC2H OLD.

THE SAD SOUND

The E Minor Chord

UP TO now you've been playing fairly sprightly tunes, with happy sounding melodies (the words of *Banks of the Ohio* not withstanding). But music can also sound sad or sinister too. Positive tunes usually use what are known as *major keys;* sad or plaintive tunes are usually written in a *minor key.* Every major key has two different types of related minor keys. You don't need to bother about how they are achieved here. All you need to know is that the effect of a minor key, or even just a minor chord or two, is quite striking. Minor chords occur quite naturally within their related key without the piece necessarily having to be written in the minor key.

In Bob Dylan's classic *Blowin' in the Wind,* you will find just such an example – a fourth chord, E minor, cropping up among the three other chords of the G family that you have already learned – those three being major chords. Practise fingering the E minor chord until you are familiar with it and then try the exercise below. You'll hear clearly the different sound produced by the addition of E minor.

When you're changing smoothly from chord to chord have a crack at *Blowin' in the Wind.* (This song appears later in a slightly tarted up version that will make it sound more interesting).

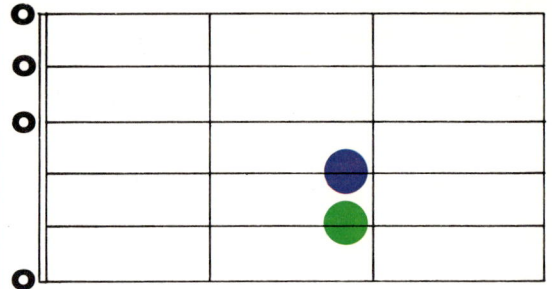

| Em | G | D |

| C | Em | C | D |

| Em | G | Em | C | D | G |

BLOWIN' IN THE WIND

G / / / / / **C** / / / **G** / / / / **Em** / /
How many   roads must a   man walk down

G / / / / **C** / / / **G** / / / / / /
be-fore you call him a   man?   Yes, and

C / / / / **G** / / / / **Em** / /
how many   seas must a   white dove   sail

G / / / / / **C** / / / **D** / / / / /
be-fore she   sleeps in the   sand?

G / / / / **C** / / / **G** / / / / /
Yes, and how many   times must the can-non

Em / / / **G** / / / **C** / / / /
balls   fly   be-fore they are for-ev-er

D / / / / / **C** / / / / **D** /
banned?   The an-swer, my friend,

G / / / / / **Em** / /
is   blowin' in the wind,

C / / / / / **D** / / / **G** / / / / / /
the an-swer is   blowin' in the wind.

Bob Dylan (right), *prophet of folk-rock, started out as a coffee-bar singer in Greenwich Village, New York.*

2. How many times must a man look up before he can see the sky?
Yes, and how many ears must one man have before he can hear people cry?
Yes, and how many deaths will it take 'till he knows that too many people have died?
The answer, my friend, is blowin' in the wind, the answer is blowin' in the wind.

3. How many years can a mountain exist before it is washed to the sea?
Yes, and how many years can some people exist before they're allowed to be free?
Yes, and how many times can a man turn his head pretendin' he just doesn't see?
The answer, my friend, is blowin' in the wind, the answer is blowin' in the wind.

TABLATURE TELLS ALL

SOONER OR later you'll begin to hanker for a string of single notes (an *arpeggio*) to make up the melody or tune. Don't be put off by the term 'arpeggio'; it is merely another name for a broken chord. Chords can be played with all the notes sounded simultaneously, in which case they are called 'chords'; or with the notes of the chord spread out and played in succession, when they are known as 'arpeggios'. As a result, the chord (D, G, C or whatever) is named at the start of the arpeggio as if it were a chord played vertically.

To play arpeggios you don't *have* to learn musical notation, although it helps. Here an easy-to-follow system known as *tablature* comes to the rescue. This is how it works.

Each of the six lines represents a string on the guitar. The nut is on your left as you look at it. The top line is the first string, the thinnest and highest in sound (E). The bottom line is the sixth string – the one nearest your chin! – which is the lowest in sound (E two octaves below top E).

The number written through the line (that is, the string) tells you what to do with your *left hand*, i.e. which *fret* of that string to press. The figure '0' through the line means that you play that string open, without fretting it. The arrows

Opposite: *Loudon Wainwright, guitarist, singer and songwriter wins his audience with livelier-than-live performances and wry humour.*

relate to your *right hand.* They show the direction in which you run your thumb (or pick) across the strings from the sixth, fifth, or fourth string as indicated. The red arrows pointing *upwards* show *down* strums. And *downward* blue arrows show *up* strums – you'll come to these later. One last thing: the divisions on the tablature indicate bars, as in conventional music.

Tablature Exercise

Finger a G chord with your left hand. The figure 3 on the bottom line of the tablature is the 3rd fret of the sixth string. The figure 2 on the line above it is the 2nd fret on the fifth string. As you hold down the G chord you will see that you are already pressing those two frets.

Now concentrate on your right hand. With your thumb or a flatpick (plectrum) pluck the sixth string (which you are already fretting at the 3rd fret), and at the same time say 'One' out loud. Then brush down on the other five strings of your G chord and say 'Two' out loud. Now pluck the fifth string (which you are holding down at the 2nd fret) and say 'Three' out loud; then brush down on the four top strings of the G chord and say 'Four'. When you've done this, change to E Minor and continue the exercise.

FLATPICKING

NOW YOU'RE just about ready for a stab at *Cottonfields*, another Beach Boys hit in the traditional style, following in the footsteps of the great Leadbelly. This song gets you started on very simple flat-picking. The technique forms the basis of many country songs and instrumentals. It consists of picking a single note with the plectrum then strumming down or sometimes up across the strings of the associated chord.

Play *Cottonfields* exactly as you did the exercise, with the same count of four beats to each bar. (A 'bar' is merely a regular measure of music.) Watch the first bar in *Cottonfields,* above the words 'When I'. This amounts to only half a bar, for which you count 'Three, four'.

Below: *Leadbelly (Huddie Ledbetter) legendary blues musician and king of the 12-string guitar.*

COTTONFIELDS

G ... C
When I was a biddy little baby my mother would rock me in the

G ... D
cra — dle in them old ———— cot — ton fields back home. ————

G ... C
When I was a biddy little baby my mother would rock me in the

38

G cra—dle in them old ———— cot—ton fields back home. ————

C Now when them cot—ton bols got rot—ten you couldn't pick very much

cot—ton in them old ———— cot—ton fields back home. ———— **D**

G It was down in Louisi ———— an—a just a-bout a mile from Tex—ar— **C**

G —ka—na in them old ———————— cot—ton fields back home. ———————— **D** **G**

2.   It may sound a little bit funny but you didn't make very much money,
In them old cottonfields back home. (REPEAT)

CHORUS

3.   I was home in Arkansas people ask me what you come here for,
In them old cottonfields back home. (REPEAT)

CHORUS

G When I was a bid-dy lit-tle ba-by my moth-er would rock me in the **C** cra—dle in them **G**

old cot—ton fields back home. When I was a bid-dy lit-tle **D** **G**

ba-by my moth-er would rock me in the crad-le in them old cot-ton fi—elds back **C** **G**

home. Now when them cot—ton bols got rot—ten you could n't pick ver-y much **G** **C** **G**

cot—ton in them old cot-ton fi—elds back home. It was **D**

down in Lou-is—i ——an-a just a—bout a mile from Tex-ar —— ka—na in them old **G** **C** **G**

cot—ton fi—elds back home. 2. It may home **G**

Words and music by Huddie Ledbetter. © 1962 Folkways Music Pub. Inc., assigned to Kensington Music Ltd., Essex House, 19/20 Poland Street, London W1V 3DD. Reproduced by kind permission of Kensington Music Ltd.

YOU CAN get pretty tired of the 'oompah' sound (picking a single bass string and following it with a couple of strummed chords) after you've played it over and over again for an hour or two. You can vary the pattern by slipping in a bass run here and there. Instead of playing the strummed chord you play one or two single notes (going up or down) to link one chord with another. Here are a few bass runs you can use in the key of G. Try each one separately and then try combining them.

G to E Minor: Play the second fret of the sixth string with the index finger of your left hand

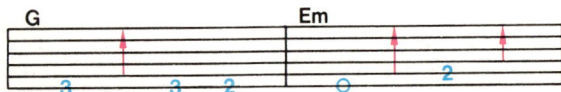

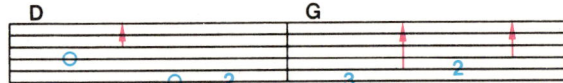

G | Em

G to D: Play the second fret of the fifth string with the index finger and the third fret of the fifth string with the ring finger of your left hand

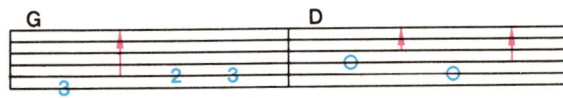

G | D

G to C: Play the second fret of the fifth string with the ring finger of your left hand

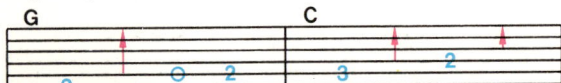

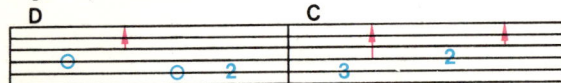

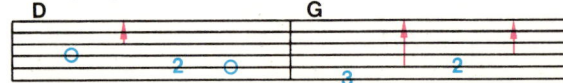

G | C

D to G: Play the second fret of the sixth string with the index finger of your left hand

D | G

D to C: Play the second fret of the fifth string with the ring finger of your left hand

D | C

D to G (alternative): Play the second fret of the fifth string with the ring finger of your left hand

D | G

BLOWIN' IN THE WIND (2)

WHEN YOU have practised these runs sufficiently to be able to play them smoothly you can have a go at a slightly more advanced version of *Blowin' in the Wind* which you met in earlier pages. Use the same style as you did in *Cottonfields.* You'll find that the bass runs linking some of the chords add more interest to the song. Don't over-emphasize these runs, or the song will sound disjointed. They sound best when subtly blended into the accompaniment. So play them cool.

Right: *Bob Dylan in reflective mood.*

G | C | G | Em

How — many roads must a man — walk down be —

G | C | G

fore you — call — him a man? Yes, and

C   **G**   **Em**

how — man y   seas   must a   white   dove —   sail —— be —

G   **C**   **D**

fore —— she   sleeps   in the   sand?   Yes, and

G   **C**   **G**   **Em**

how — man y   times   must the   can-non   balls   fly —— be —

G   **C**   **D**

fore   they are   for — ev — er   banned? ——————CHORUS The

C   **D**   **G**   **Em**

an —— swer, my   friend, —— is   blowin'   in the   wind,   the

C   **D**   **G**

an —— swer is   blowin'   in the   wind. ——————————

2.   How many times must a man look up before he can see the sky?
     Yes, and how many ears must one man have before he can hear people cry?
     Yes, and how many deaths will it take 'till he knows that too many people have died?
     The answer, my friend, is blowin' in the wind, the answer is blowin' in the wind.

3.   How many years can a mountain exist before it is washed to the sea?
     Yes, and how many years can some people exist before they're allowed to be free?
     Yes, and how many times can a man turn his head pretendin' he just doesn't see?
     The answer, my friend, is blowin' in the wind, the answer is blowin' in the wind.

G   **C**   **G**   **Em**   **G**

How many   roads must a   man walk — down   be —— fore— you

C   **G**   **C**

call him a   man? —————— Yes, and   how man—y   seas must a

G   **Em**   **G**   **C**   **D**

white dove — sail   be ——fore — she   sleeps in the   sand? ——

G   **C**   **D**   **G**   **Em**   **C**

Yes, and   how man—y   times must the   can-non balls — fly   be —

D   **G**   **Em**   **C**   **D**

— fore they are   for — ev — er   banned? —— CHORUS The   an — swer, my

G

friend, is   blowin' in the   wind,   the   an — swer is   blowin' in the

G

wind. ——————

FINGERPICKIN' GOOD

NOW IS the time to exercise those right hand fingers and show what they can do. The standard way of using these is for the thumb to pick the three bass strings (4, 5, and 6) and for the index finger to pick the third string, the middle finger to pick the second string, and the ring finger to look after the first string. There are all sorts of exceptions to these rules but you can forget about them for the time being.

Three Exercises

The first one is written in 3/4 (waltz) time. This means that you count three beats in each bar, and not four as in *Cottonfields* and *Blowin' in the Wind*. Hold down a G chord, then with the thumb of your right hand pluck the sixth string. Then pluck the third string with your index finger, and

then the second string with your middle finger. Count 'One, two, three' out loud as you play these notes. Play through the rest of the exercise and practise until it flows smoothly.

The second exercise is like the first except for the time value of the notes, which is half that of the first. This means that instead of playing three notes to the bar you play six. So when you play this exercise count 'One and two and three and' out loud for each bar.

In the final exercise we're back to four beats in the bar. Remember to count out loud until you completely get the hang of it. Halfway through the exercise you'll see that the time value of each note has been halved, as in the previous exercise. So instead of playing four notes to each bar you play eight. The count per bar is 'One and two and three and four and'.

MY LADY'S A WILD FLYING DOVE

WHEN YOU feel that you've really got this finger-picking together, see what you can do with Tom Paxton's beautiful ballad *My Lady's a Wild Flying Dove*. The fingerpicking for this version is the same as you used in the second half of the last exercise (eight notes to a bar). As you pick, try and get some light and shade into your playing. You will find that a fairly simple accompaniment becomes really worth listening to.

Tom Paxton (right) *keeps his music simple.*

Some la——dies are fool——ish   Some la——dies are gay.

Some la——dies are come——ly   Some live while they may.

CHORUS   My la——dy's a wild fly-ing dove   my la——dy is wine.

She whis——pers each eve———ning   she's mine, mine, mine,

2. She likes pretty pictures
   She loves singing birds
   She'll watch them for hours
   But I see only her.

   CHORUS

3. She tells me she's learning
   How full her cup can be
   She asks me to help her
   But I know she teaches me.

   CHORUS

1. Some la——dies are fool——ish   Some la——dies are gay.   Some lad——ies are

come———ly   Some live while they may.   CHORUS My la——dy's a wild fly—in' dove

my la——dy is wine.   She whis——pers each eve——ning she's mine, mine,

mine.

Words and music by Tom Paxton. © 1965 Cherry Lane Music Inc., assigned to Harmony Music Ltd., Essex House, 19/20 Poland Street, London W1V 3DD. Reproduced by kind permission of Harmony Music Ltd.

YOU ALREADY know the C chord: here are the other main chords of the group – G Seventh, F Major and A Minor – laid out in tablature. We'll come to the special chord (below right) in just a moment.

The short exercise on the next page is flatpicking in 3/4 time. Hold down a C chord then pluck the fifth string. At the same time count 'One', and then strum downwards across the four top strings twice, counting 'Two' on the first strum and 'Three' on the second. Now play through the rest of the first part of this exercise.

In the second part of the exercise you have four short strums in each bar. Hold down a C chord with your left hand and pluck the fifth string. As you do this, count 'One and'. Then strum down and up across the top four strings counting 'Two and'. Repeat the down and up strum across the strings counting 'Three and'. Now continue through the exercise.

You are now ready to have a go at Peter Sarstedt's *Where Do You Go To My Lovely?* which appears on pages 46–47. The song uses a special chord – for that special sound – marked 1 . This chord is actually 'G Suspended Seventh' and is merely an unusual way of playing G7

Peter Sarstedt (below) *had only one hit–the haunting* Where do you go to my lovely?

The G7 Chord

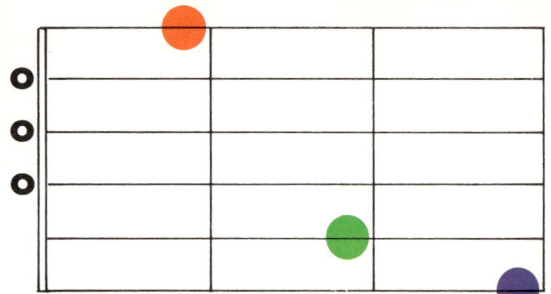

The Gsus7 Chord ①

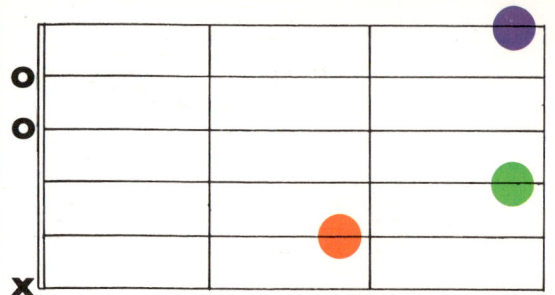

The F Chord

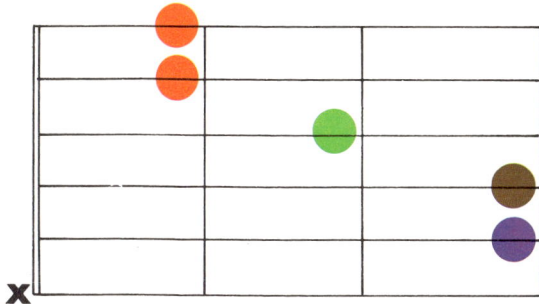

The A Minor Chord

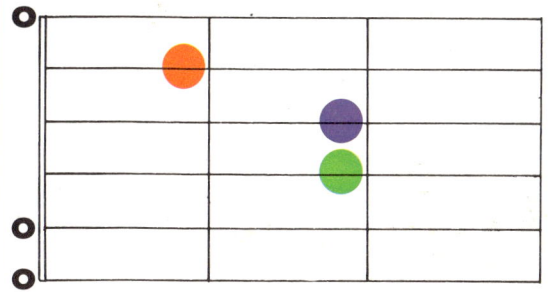

1

C   F

COUNT: one   two   three   one   two   three etc.

G^7 C

2

C   Am   F

one and two and three and   one and two and three and   one and two and three and

G^7 C

45

WHERE DO YOU GO TO MY LOVELY

C ... **Em**

You talk —— like Mar — len — e Deit — rich ——

F ... **G**

And you dance like Zi Zi Jean Maire

C ... **Em**

Your clothes are all made by Bal — ma — in

F ... **G**

And there's dia — monds and pearls in your hair, yes there

① **Em** **G⁷**

are. 2. You live —— in a

Em ... **F**

fan — cy a —— part — ment Off the Bou — le — vard

G ... **C**

of St Mi —— chel Where you keep —— your

Em ... **F**

Roll — ing Stones re — cords —— And a friend of

G ① **Em**

Sach - a Dis —— tel, yes you do.

G⁷ **C** **Em**

CHORUS But where do you go to my love – ly

F ... **G**

When you're a —— lone in your bed

C **Em**

Tell me the thoughts that sur —— round you

46

Em — i want to look in — side your head, yes I

F **G**

(1) do 3. I've

Em **G7** [continue with remaining verses & choruses]

G FINAL CHORUS **C**

in — side your head _____ .

3. I've seen all your qualifications
   You got from the Sorbonne,
   And the painting you stole from Picasso,
   Your loveliness goes on and on, yes it does.

4. When you go on your summer vacation,
   You go to Juan le Pain,
   With your carefully designed topless swimsuit,
   You get an even suntan, on your back and on your legs.

CHORUS

5. And when the snow falls you're found in St. Moritz,
   With the others of the jet-set,
   And you sip your Napoleon brandy,
   But you never get your lips wet, no you don't.

6. Your name it is heard in high places,
   You know the Aga Khan,
   He sent you a racehorse for Christmas,
   And you keep it just for fun, for a laugh, ha ha ha.

CHORUS

7. They say that when you get married,
   It'll be to a millionaire,
   But they don't realise where you come from,
   And I wonder if they really care, or give a damn.

8. I remember the back streets of Naples,
   Two children begging in rags,
   Both touched with a burning ambition,
   To shake off their lowly born tags, and they try.

CHORUS

9. So look into my face Marie-Claire,
   And remember just who you are,
   Then go and forget me forever,
   But I know you still bear the scar, deep inside,
   yes you do.

FINAL CHORUS:
   I know where you go to my lovely,
   When you're alone in your bed,
   I know the thoughts that surround you,
   'Cause I can look inside your head.

C You talk like Mar — len — e Deit ——— rich **Em** And you

F dance like Zi Zi Jean Maire **G** Your clothes are. **C**

Em all made by Bal ——— main And there's dia — monds and pearls in your **F**

G hair, yes there are. **Em** 2. You live in a **C**

fan — cy a ——— part — ment Off the Bou — le — vard of St Mi — **Em** **F**

G chel Where you keep your Roll — ing Stones re — cords **C**

F And a friend of Sach — a Dis ——— tel, yes you do. **G**

Words and music by Peter Sarstedt. © 1977 United Artists Music Ltd., Richard House, 30-32 Mortimer Street, London W1A 2JL.

FINGERPICKING BASS RUNS AND HARMONICS

YOU SHOULD know all about bass runs by now, but harmonics are something new. There's nothing frightening about them and they do add polish to your playing. Here's how they're done.

Lay the little finger of your left hand flat but *very lightly* across the first string at the 12th fret. Place your finger right on the metal fret instead of just behind it, and barely touch the string so that the string is free to vibrate. Now pick the first string with a right hand finger. The effect should be a sweet, high-pitched, chiming sound. If it sounds muffled, you're pressing too hard. Try it on other strings, all at the 12th fret.

The traditional melody, *Scarborough Fair,* popularized by Simon and Garfunkel, takes harmonics in its stride. They are marked Hx and you will, in fact, find yourself fretting three strings at once at the 12th fret. In this version of the song the fingerpicking style is the same as the one you used in the second fingerpicking exercise. The count for each bar is 'One and two and three and' ie. six notes to the bar — one count for each note played. Remember?

Below: *Paul Simon's music and lyrics made a perfect blend with Art Garfunkel's soprano vocals.*

SCARBOROUGH FAIR

Em   **G**   **D**   **Em**

Are you go-ing to Scar —— bor-ough Fair.

G   **Em**   **Em**   **Am**

Pars —— ley, sage, rose —— ma —— ry and

Em

thyme.   Re —— mem —— ber

G   **Em**   **D**

me to one who lives th —— ere.

Em   **D**   **Em**

She once was a true love of mine.

2. Tell her to make me a cambric shirt
   Parsley, sage, rosemary and thyme.
   Without any seams nor needle work
   Then she'll be a true love of mine.

3. Tell her to find me an acre of land
   Parsley, sage, rosemary and thyme.
   Between the salt water and the sea strand
   Then she'll be a true love of mine.

4. Tell her to reap it with a sickle of leather
   Parsley, sage, rosemary and thyme.
   And gather it all in a bunch of heather
   Then she'll be a true love of mine.

Em   **G**   **D**   **Em**

Are you go — ing to Scar - bor —ough Fair.

G   **Em**   **Am**

Pars – ley, sage, rose —— ma —ry and thyme.

G   **Em**

Re —— mem —ber me to one who lives th —ere. ——

Em   **D**   **Em**

—— She once was a true love of mine. ——

HAMMERING ON

HAMMERING ON is another effective trick of the trade that takes very little practice. It is merely a way of accenting or emphasizing certain notes and playing them with your left hand instead of your right. You do this by fretting a string so hard that it makes a sound.

Try this: play the second string open with your right hand index finger. Then immediately come down hard with the middle finger of your left hand on the 2nd fret of the same string. The sound of the note should come out clearly. Practise this until it does. Try it with different fingers on different strings and frets. Each hammer is marked with an H in the tablature.

Meet the Chord of D Minor

Another chord commonly used with the chords of C is D Minor. Practise playing it, then try changing to and from the other chords of C Major (G7, F, Am) until the movement is smooth and effortless. D Minor, together with some hammering on is used in *Morning Has Broken*. The right hand technique is the same as that for *Scarborough Fair*: fingerpicking in 6/4 time.

Below: *Cat Stevens dreamed up the musical setting for Eleanor Farjeon's poem* Morning Has Broken.

The D Minor Chord

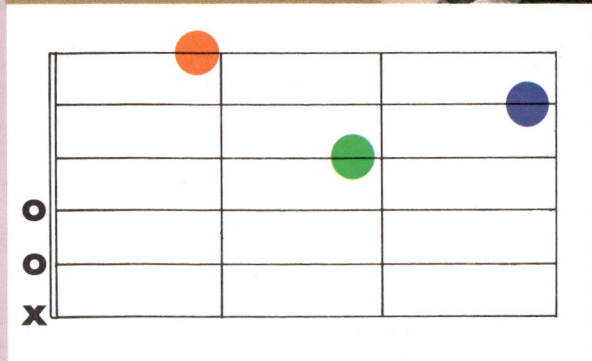

MORNING HAS BROKEN

Morn — ing has brok — en like the first morn — ing, black – bird has spok — en like the first bird.

Praise for the sing — ing, Praise for the morn — ing, Praise for them spring — ing fresh from — the world.

2. Sweet the rain's new fall, sunlit from heaven,
Like the first dew-fall on the first grass.
Praise for the sweetness of the wet garden,
Sprung in completeness where his feet pass.

3. Mine is the sunlight, mine is the morning,
Born of the one light Eden saw play.
Praise with elation, praise every morning,
God's re-creation of the new day.

REPEAT FIRST VERSE

Morn-ing has brok — en like the first morn — ing, black bird has spok — en like the first bird. Praise for the sing — ing, Praise for the morn — ing, Praise for them spring — ing fresh from — the world.

Words by Eleanor Farjeon, musical arrangement by Cat Stevens. © 1971 Freshwater Music Ltd., 47 British Grove, London W4.

BASIC CLAWHAMMER

CLAWHAMMER IS playing eight notes to the bar with alternate picking of a bass string with a treble string. Follow the exercise carefully before attempting John Denver's *Leaving on a Jet Plane.* It can be a rewarding piece when played properly.

Right: American singer/songwriter, John Denver leans hard on boyish charm.

G
one and two and three and four and

Em
one and two and three and four and

one and two and three and four and

one and two and three and four and etc.

C   D

G   F   Am   G

LEAVING ON A JET PLANE

D   G   C   G

All my bags are packed, I'm — ready to — go, I'm stand—ing here out —

C   G   C   D

— side your — door, — I hate to wake you up to say — good———bye.

D   G   C   G

But the dawn is break—in', it's ear—ly morn, the tax — i's wait—in' he's

C   G   C   D

blowin' his horn. Al ———ready I'm so lone—some I could die.

52

CHORUS So kiss me and smile for me, ——— tell me that you'll wait for me, hold me like you'll nev—er let me go.

'Cause I'm leav———in' on a jet plane, don't know when I'll be back a–gain Oh babe, I hate to go.

2. There's so many times I've let you down;
So many times I've played around,
I tell you now they don't mean a thing.
Every place I go I'll think of you,
Every song I sing I'll sing for you.
When I come back I'll bring your wedding ring.

3. Now the time has come to leave you,
One more time let me kiss you,
Then close your eyes, I'll be on my way.
Dream about the days to come,
When I won't have to leave alone,
About the time I won't have to say.

CHORUS (after each verse):
So kiss me and smile for me, tell me that you'll wait for me,
Hold me like you'll never let me go.
'Cause I'm leavin' on a jet plane, don't know when I'll be back again.
Oh babe, I hate to go.

All my bags are packed, I'm ready to go, I'm standing here out——side your door, I hate to wake you up to say —— good ——— bye. But the dawn is break—in' it's ear—ly morn, the tax–i's waitin' he's blowin' his horn. Al——ready I'm so lonesome I could die. —— CHORUS So kiss me and smile for me, —— tell me that you'll wait for me, —— hold me like you'll never let me go. Cause I'm leav———in', on a jet plane, don't know when I'll be back a–gain Oh babe, I hate to —— go. ——— 2. There's so

Words and music by John Denver. © 1967 & 1971 Cherry Lane Music Inc., assigned to Harmony Music Ltd., Essex House, 19/20 Poland Street, London W1V 3DD. Reproduced by kind permission of Harmony Music Ltd.

The A Chord

The F#m7 Chord

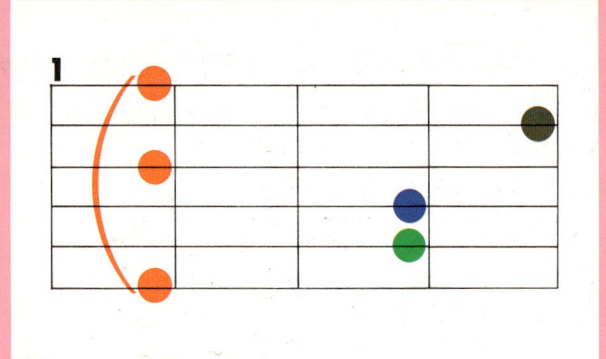

The E Chord

The B Chord

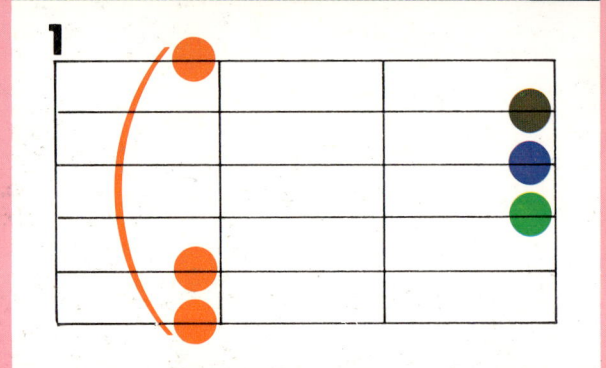

THE CHORDS at near left (F Sharp Minor Seventh and B Major) are *barré* chords. You may find them a bit tricky to start with, but after some practice they'll come as easy as the others. If you look at the picture and tablature you'll see that it is a question of laying your finger along the line. To start with practise the barré on its own. For a clear sound tilt your finger to the left so that the bony edge presses on the strings.

When you can play the barré on its own reasonably well, add the other notes to make up the chord of F Sharp Minor Seventh. Do the same with the B Major chord, then practise changing back and forth from one to the other.

When you've got the hang of these barré chords you'll find it easy to learn the chords of E Major and A Major. With these chords at your fingertips you'll enjoy playing *We Shall Overcome* (next page). This has been used as a protest song and signature tune for hundreds of thousands of demonstrators, and has been sung by artists such as Joan Baez and Peter Seeger. Based on an old hymn, the tune should be performed solemnly, each full chord being strummed through strongly and clearly with the thumb or a pick.

Below: *Singer Joan Baez has long been active in Civil Rights and human rights campaigns.*

WE SHALL OVERCOME

Slowly, in march time

We shall o — ver — come, ——————— We shall o — ver —

come, ——————— We shall o — ver — come — some

day. ——————— Oh, —— deep —— in my

heart, ——————— I — do be — lieve ——————— that

we shall o — ver — come — some ——————— day. ———————

2. We'll walk hand in hand, we'll walk hand in hand,
We'll walk hand in hand, some day.
Oh, deep in my heart I do believe
That we shall overcome some day.

Additional verses
We shall live in peace . . .
The truth will make us free . . .
We shall brothers be . . .

We shall o — ver — come, ——— We shall o — ver — come,

We shall o — ver —— come some ——— day. ——— Oh, ———

deep in my ——— heart, ——— I do be — lieve ——— that

we shall o — ver —— come some ——— day. ———————

NOW YOU'RE going to do some real clawhammer fingerpicking. You'll notice in the tablature of the next two exercises that you've got to hold the first note of each bar for twice as long as the other notes. There are also a couple of places in the second exercise where the picking is varied by playing bass and treble strings together. The timing is still the same as in the first exercise.

Your chance to show off this new style comes on the next pages in the popular ballad *Streets of London*, by Ralph McTell (pictured above). The song carries an instrumental break, which is played at the end of each chorus. This instrumental break is written out in tablature, and you'll find it similar to the accompaniment of the verse, *not* the chorus.

one and two and three and four   one and two and three and four   and etc.

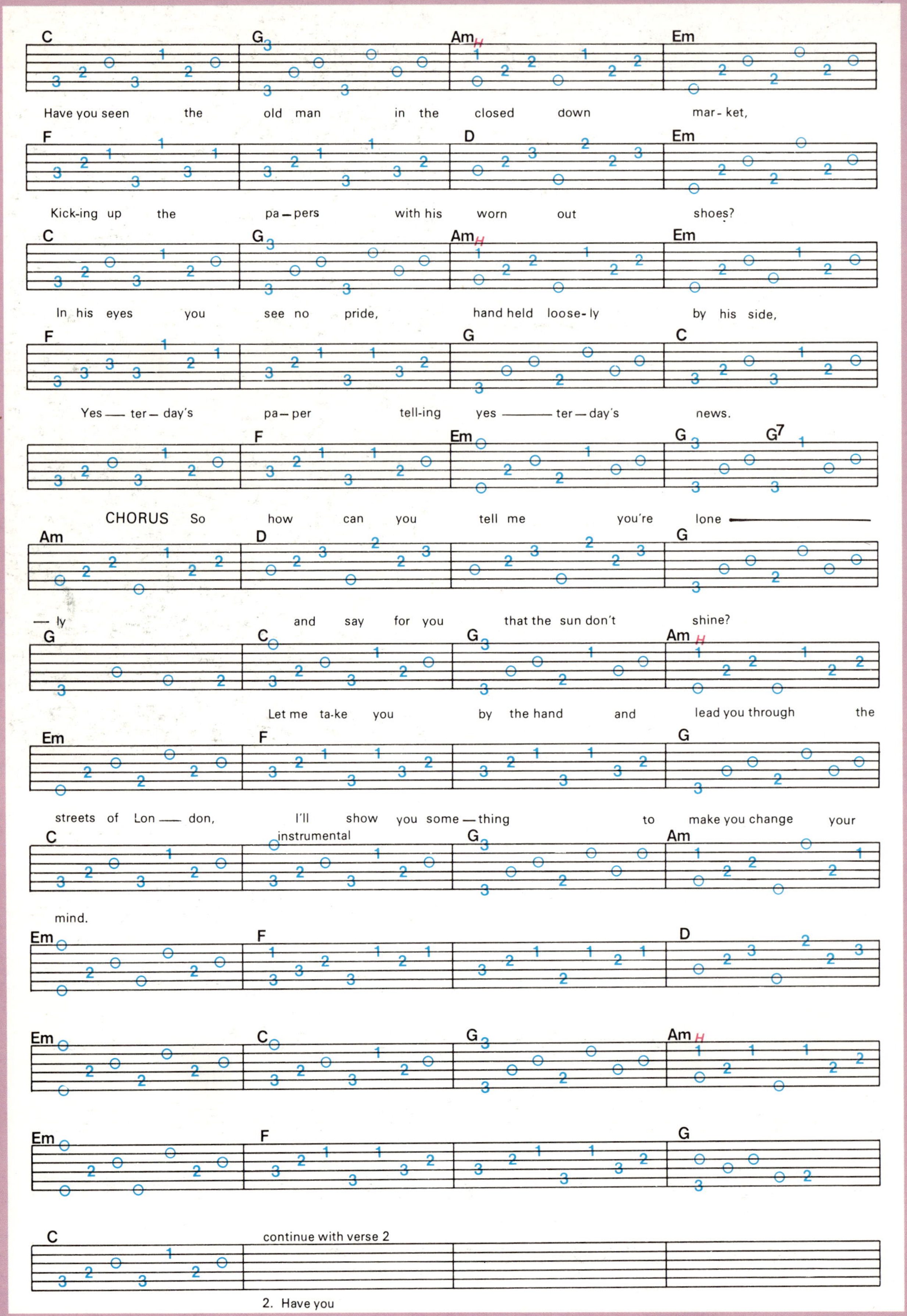

C · G · Am · Em
Have you seen the old man in the closed down mar-ket,

F · D · Em
Kick-ing up the pa—pers with his worn out shoes?

C · G · Am · Em
In his eyes you see no pride, hand held loose-ly by his side,

F · G · C
Yes—ter—day's pa—per tell-ing yes———ter—day's news.

F · Em · G · G7
CHORUS So how can you tell me you're lone————

Am · D · G
— ly and say for you that the sun don't shine?

G · C · G · Am
Let me ta-ke you by the hand and lead you through the

Em · F · G
streets of Lon——don, I'll show you some—thing to make you change your

C · G · Am
mind. instrumental

Em · F · D

Em · C · G · Am

Em · F · G

C
continue with verse 2

2. Have you

STREETS OF LONDON

2. Have you seen the old girl who walks the streets of London,
   Dirt in her hair and her clothes in rags?
   She's no time for talkin', she just keeps right on walkin',
   Carrying her home in two carrier bags.

CHORUS

3. In the all night cafe at a quarter past eleven
   Same old man sitting there on his own.
   Looking at the world over the rim of his tea cup.
   Each tea lasts an hour and he wanders home alone.

CHORUS

4. Have you seen the old man outside the seaman's mission,
   Memory fading with the medal ribbon that he wears?
   In our winter city the rain cries a little pity
   For one more forgotten hero in a world that doesn't care.

CHORUS

Right: *Ex-busker Ralph McTell's playing style is based on gentle ragtime music.*

Have you seen the old man in the closed down mar — ket, Kick-ing up — the pa—pers with his worn out shoes? In his eyes you see no pride, hand held loose — ly by his side, Yes-ter—day's paper telling yes—ter—day's news. CHORUS So how can you tell me you're lone — — ly and say for you that the sun don't shine? Let me ta—ke you by the hand and lead you through the streets of Lon—don, I'll show you some—thing to make you change your mind.

THE LAST THING ON MY MIND

TOM PAXTON'S haunting refrain, *The Last Thing on My Mind,* happens to be the last song in this book. There are no new chords, so you can concentrate on the right hand work. This involves flatpicking with bass runs and hammering-on. The instrumental section follows the tune of the verse and should be played after each chorus.

Not Really the End . . .

You've come almost to the end of the book but no guitarist ever stops learning and the quickest way to progress is to watch the professionals and listen to them on record. Try to figure out exactly what they're doing. Buy yourself a more advanced instruction manual, study and *practise.*

Right: *Blind guitar wizard José Feliciano recorded an evocative version of* The Last Thing on My Mind.

G | C | G

It's a les-son too late for the lear —— ning

C | G | D | G

made of sand, made of sand

| C | G

In the wink of an eye my soul is turn — ing

C | G | D | G

in your hand, in your hand

| | | D | | | C

CHORUS Are you go-ing a —— way with no word of fare ——

G | C | D

—well? Will there be not a trace left be —— hind?

Well I could have loved you bet-ter, did—n't mean to be un——kind. You know that was the last thing on my mind.

instrumental

2. You've got reason a plenty for going,
This I know, this I know.
For the weeds have been steadily growing,
Please don't go, please don't go.

CHORUS

3. As I lie in my bed in the morning,
Without you, without you.
Each song in my breast dies a borning,
Without you, without you.

CHORUS

It's a les—son too late for the lear——ning made of sand, made of sand In the wink of an eye my soul is turn—ing in your hand, in your hand CHORUS Are you go——ing a—way with no word of fare——well? Will there be not a trace left be——hind? Well I could have loved you bet-ter, did-n't mean to be un——kind. You know that was the last thing on my mind.

Words and music by Tom Paxton. © 1964 & 1973 Deep Fork Music Inc., assigned to Harmony Music Ltd., Essex House, 19/20 Poland Street, London W1V 3DD. Reproduced by kind permission of Harmony Music Ltd.

CHORD CHART

Here is a clear and comprehensive chord chart that puts a wide variety of sounds instantly at your fingertips. With this at-a-glance guide you'll be able to play hundreds of popular songs

Major

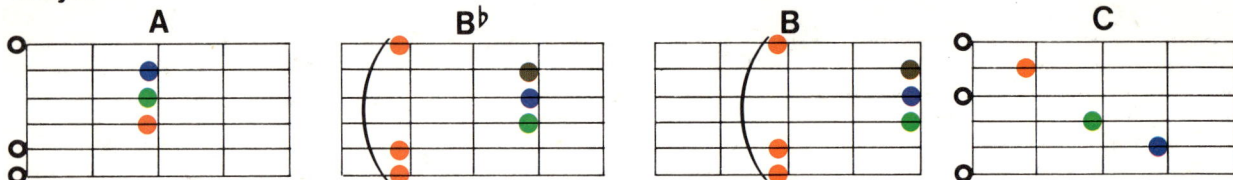

A   B♭   B   C

Minor

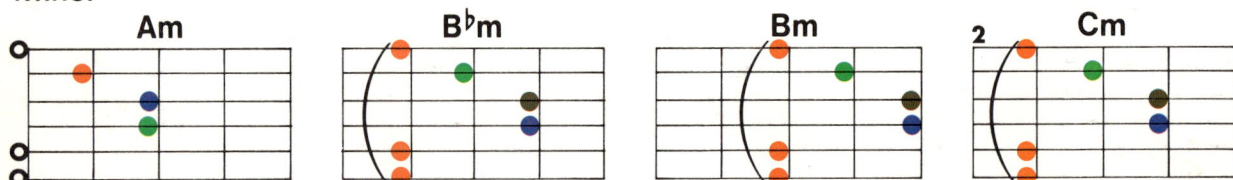

Am   B♭m   Bm   Cm

Dominant 7th

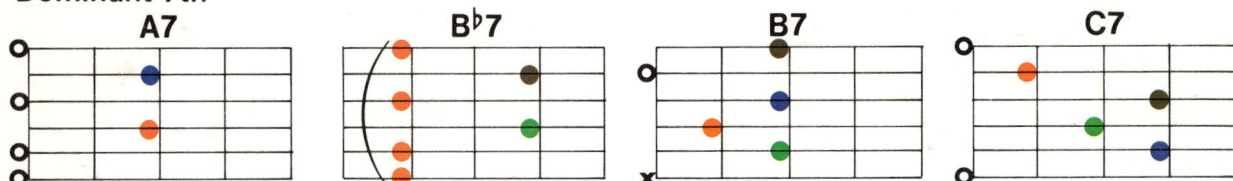

A7   B♭7   B7   C7

Minor 7th

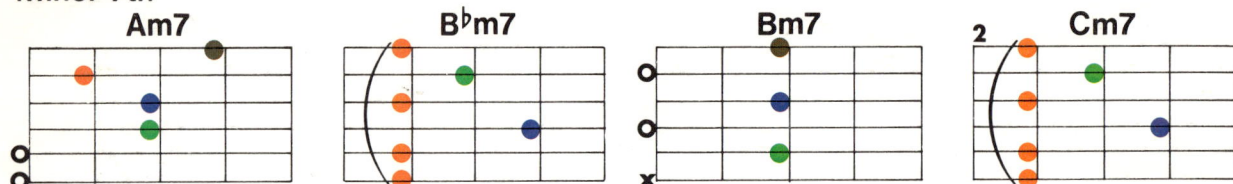

Am7   B♭m7   Bm7   Cm7

Added 6th

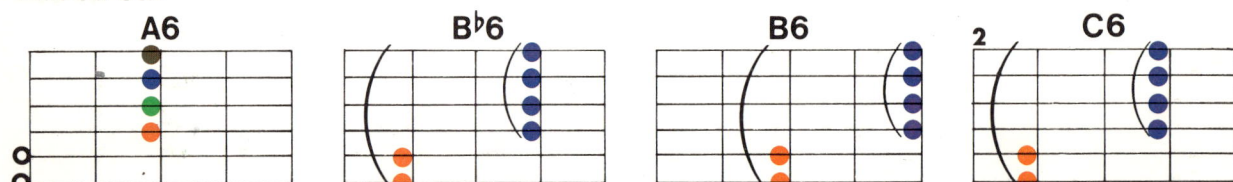

A6   B♭6   B6   C6

Minor 6th

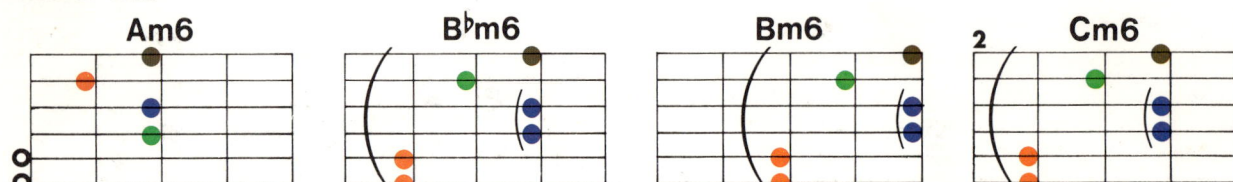

Am6   B♭m6   Bm6   Cm6

Major 7th

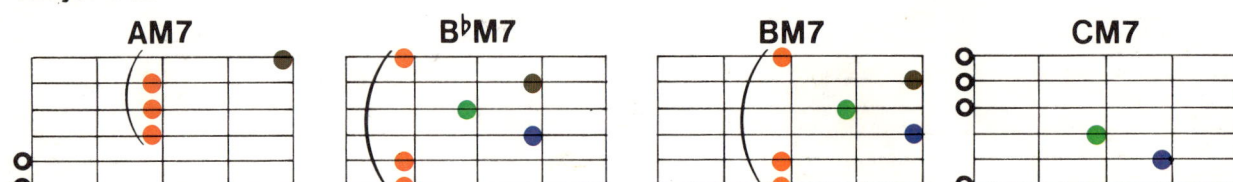

AM7   B♭M7   BM7   CM7

in both major and minor keys. Practise any unfamiliar chords — the fingering on some is quite tricky — until you can play them as smoothly as those you have already mastered.

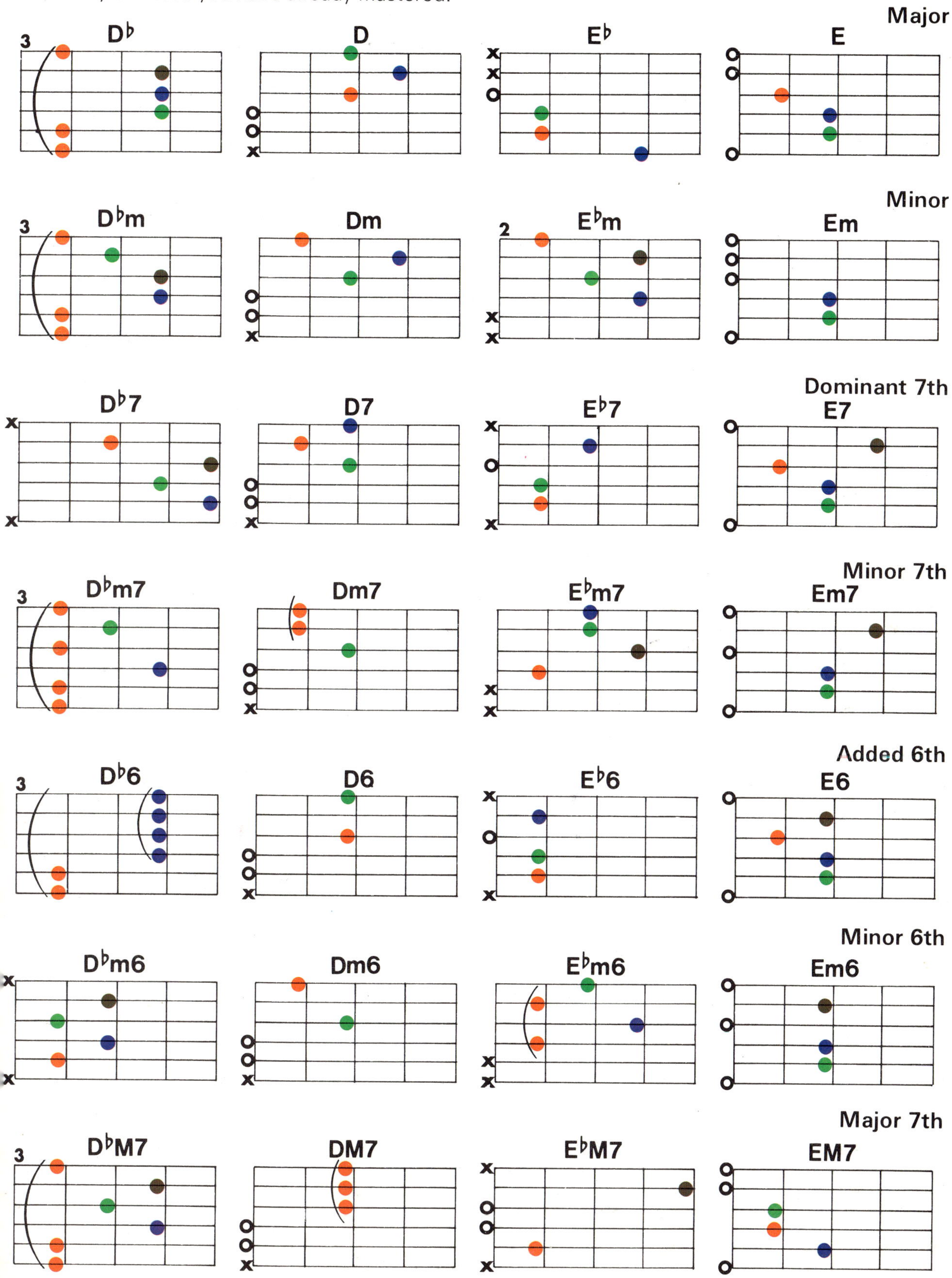

Major

D♭ D E♭ E

Minor

D♭m Dm E♭m Em

Dominant 7th

D♭7 D7 E♭7 E7

Minor 7th

D♭m7 Dm7 E♭m7 Em7

Added 6th

D♭6 D6 E♭6 E6

Minor 6th

D♭m6 Dm6 E♭m6 Em6

Major 7th

D♭M7 DM7 E♭M7 EM7

Major

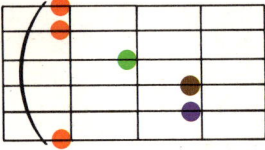

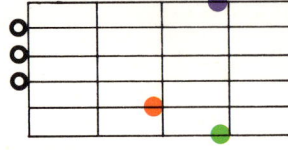

Minor

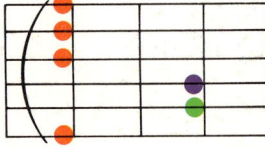
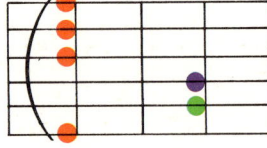

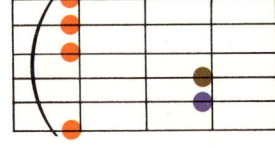

Dominant 7th

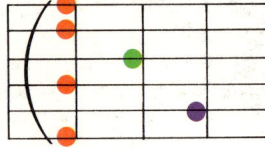

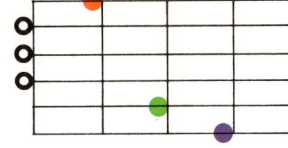

Minor 7th

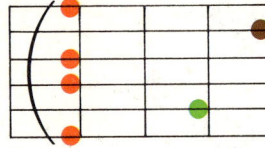
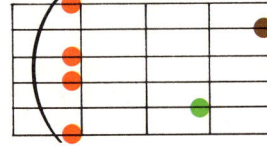

Added 6th

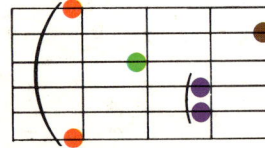
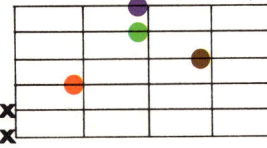

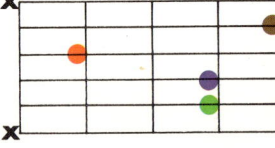

Minor 6th

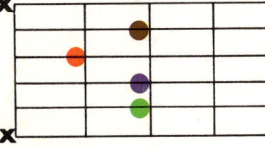

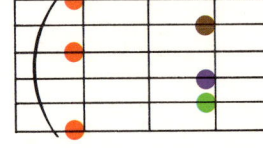

Major 7th

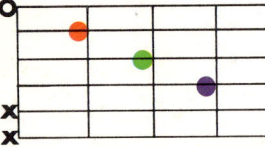
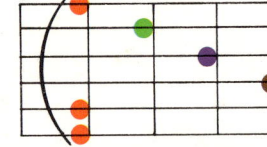
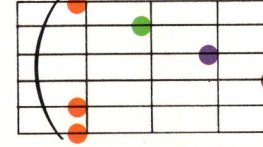

Published by The Hamlyn Publishing Group Limited; London ● New York ● Sydney ● Toronto ● Astronaut House, Feltham, Middlesex, England. ISBN 0 600 37178 6.